The Promise of Memory

Michael Weeder

African Perspectives Publishing
PO Box 95342, Grant Park 2051, South Africa
www.africanperspectives.co.za

PRINT: ISBN 978-1-990976-76-6
DIGITAL: ISBN 978-1-990976-77-3

Cover Image: Jimi Matthews
Editor: Diana Ferrus
Graphic Designer: Roxy Conradie
Typesetting: Phumzile Mondlani

CONTENTS

Introduction

I first met Michael Weeder in London in 1982, when our braided paths intersected in Brixton, the UK capital city's cultural and political heartbeat. Our encounter was less a product of fortuity than the guided harmony of divine providence. Just like Linton Kwesi Johnson once said in a poem that a truncheon striking a black youth in Brixton bounces off the head of another in Soweto, a scribe of the people's struggle in the burning streets of eighties Apartheid South Africa would in turn rebound onto the streets of Brixton's famous frontline.

On that summer's day, one year after the seminal 1981 Brixton uprising, Michael and I were walking from the offices of the Race Today Collective (which included Linton Kwesi Johnson). With us was a young Jamaican-born man who aggressively dismissed Michael's claim to blackness. Vacuously spouting his grossly limited perception of our people's long history of resistance to oppression, he reduced my Capetonian brother to being "just a coloured", and therefore a lesser sufferer in the iniquitous grand scheme of Apartheid.

On that occasion, the 24-year-old Michael did not possess the existential resources to meaningfully refute the Jamaican brother's challenge to the provenance of his belonging. Possibly compelled by this cardinal moment in his life, Michael would eventually grow into the vastly knowledgeable man that he now is, and become a sought-after sage to the communities seeking to know the story of their emergence as a people whose interlaced roots map a matrix of diverse routes across the East Indies, Europe and Africa.

After a few decades I reconnected with Michael – now the Very Reverend Michael Weeder, Dean of St. George's Cathedral - on

Facebook, where we would often see each other's writing about the unfolding social transformations in South Africa and the rest of the world.

Then he came to London again in 2016 bearing the deep recess in his mind from the Brixton baton that bounced off his head in the Cape of unfulfilled hopes. We met for a brunch catch-up at my favourite haunt, the Royal Festival Hall, at Southbank Centre, and made time to take a memorable photo by the world-famous Nelson Mandela bust.

And so it is with amplified feelings of honour, pleasure and pride that I write this introduction to Michael's compendium of poems, **The Promise of Memory.**

Michael's book celebrates the profundity of our shared South African history as a crucible for the improbable blending of its key inherited components of violation and veneration. It is a timely offering in its accentuation of the healing imperative of staring pain in the face with a poetic pathos of unfathomable depth, as evidenced in "Biko Part 1":

Biko, they killed your body. And we wept
at the sight of your dark, bruised and beaten beauty.
And now. All over this forsaken Azania
you, like resurrection hymns
like the promise of empty graves
like the sound of the marching poor
you come singing our forgotten songs ...

A universal human tenderness expressed through the poetic meridians of love percolates through *"September child"*, written for Chiara, his first-born daughter "who saw the light of this life in September 1986":

embracing enemy territory
sometime between
dark and dawn.

Nomalanga, our golden flower
in darkening days.

Jazz, your lullaby
freedom, your morning prayer
and Africa, our gift to you.

Promise child of what we
may never know. We bow
to the wisdom
of your generous smile,
warm and spilling
from the home of original innocence.

At this current confluence of his many rivers of experience, Weeder exudes a profoundly cultivated sense of his place in our country's long and nuanced trajectory. He is positively proud of his deeply embedded roots in the mother city's unique interwoven narrative of identity. This pride is a product of the unveiling and nurturing of his formerly stifled instinctive inner sense of belonging, which has evolved to imbue his poetry with an unmistakable pride of self. His verse flows unhindered from this wellspring of confidence, taking in a host of stylistic idioms and imagery provided by the generous curves of its navigation of life's verdant banks.

The poem '*I know where me from*' is a personal reflection that echoes the tutelage of that original encounter in Brixton in 1982 in its self-assured assertion of identity and place:

I know where me from.
I feel it in de bounce of de goema drum
tho I not know a place specifically
or me first given name genealogically.

But I know where me from
under stormy, dark sky or under de laughin' sun

It's from here or maybe over there
but I damn sure know I am so ever-near
where dem be black or brown
or honey and beige all aroun'

The artistry of Michael's poetic prowess further reveals itself in his ability to employ simplicity to portray profundity, as in "Lenten ash":

Then I saw you
whose beauty
I could not name.

I tore the poem
into little pieces.

It fell, softly
like Lenten ash,
to the ground.

Then he brings us to the brazen beauty of bardic effrontery in "Steve Bantu Biko said":

Abafundisi,
when you preach
on a Sunday
about our Friday
Saturday night sins

don't be silent
about the sin
of allowing ourselves

to be oppressed and exploited
on all and other
God's given days.

In the Zulu language we say, *"Abake babona nabayo phinde babonane."* (Those who have seen each other before will see each other again).

Eugene Skeef
14 September 2020, London, United Kingdom

Preface

I believe that the world is beautiful and that poetry, like bread, is for everyone – Roque Dalton

I was born in October 1957, nine years after the formal declaration of Apartheid with its preferential bias toward whiteness of which Afrikaners were first amongst equals. My site of birth was the Cape Peninsula Maternity Hospital on the lower slopes of Hoerikwaggo, the 'mountain in the sea.' This was the name by which my Khoekhoe forebears knew the ancient mountain that looms above the city of Camissa, our 'place of sweet waters.'

My impulse to write poetry was influenced by my curiosity about the complexities of the commonwealth of South African communities. The answers about the origin of colouredness, the particular way that we who are 'coloured' belong to the land and to each other lay, in part, cloistered in the mute bosoms of our parents. My mother, in response to the incessant nagging of my adolescent self on the theme of origins, once replied: "Do you want to know if you have white people as relatives?" The thought had never occurred to me. And for a long time, my unsatiated curiosity remained encamped at the dark wells of our history.

When I reference myself and others as 'coloured' in the collection I am making a specific claim on a history of slavery and of Khoi and San genocide: its holocaust of memory and the cauterizing of any continued evolvement into interrelatedness with the African-vast riches of our geography, with our continent and its people. 'Coloured' is an undervalued fact of a traumatized past cast in the greater mosaic of a spiritual self and a social I-and-I. One's 'coloured' self is a first-phase movement in the dance of beingness. It is accompanied by the rhythmic metre of the patois carrying the flat-crack of the whip meting out punishment and reprimand. The curfew bell that could not silence the call to prayer or our muted laughter at the incomprehensible cruelty of being human chattel, owned by others, listed in the inventory of their estate.

Part of the answer to the questions about how we belong is located in the patois and the *liedjies* we sing such as '*Hoe gaarie padjie naarie kramat toe?*' This song about the road to a shrine of a Muslim saint - is a coded, rhythmic guide to the escape routes into the mountains around the early Cape settlement. Urban enslaved people would gather in the evenings on Greenmarket Square where information would be shared in the poetics of hidden meaning. Fear of detection by informants within their ranks required communication in the form of innuendos and songs. Survival depended on subterfuge and experiences which over time bridged into memory.

And this is the archive I access as amnesia, a necessity to dull the ache as a distant, repressed pain recedes. Memory throbs into verbs, adjectives and a syntax sometimes singed by anger.

This selection of my poems – covering the years from 1980 to the present day - expresses my personal attempts at making sense of the everyday, ordinary difficulties, and the small victories of life.

This offering emphasises, sometimes in an exploratory suggestiveness, how differences should not be divisive and that they form part of the range of ways in which we belong to - and are of - each other.

I know where me from

No look like me *familia* of you
maybe so or maybe no
but I sure fit de shoe of me history
that they say is longa than de gallows rope
but it de seed of me need
that's stronga than de lion of Zion hope.

I know where me from.
I feel it in de bounce of de *goema* drum
tho I not know a place specifically
or me first given name genealogically.

But I know where me from
under stormy, dark sky or under de laughin' sun.

It's from here or maybe over there
but I damn sure know I am ever-near
where dem be black or brown
or honey and beige all aroun'

that where me from
is where love is strong
and people get along
sharing de salt of life's misery
along with de heartache and the joy
that make a lickle I-and-I a mighty we.
that's where me from
is where people ever striving to stand free
like a many river flowing into one, might sea.
I know where me from.

Written near Brixton, London, Friday 10 June 2016

1

Coloured girls

with Latina names
gipsy queens at Wembley's
en route home to Mitchells Plain
from payday jazzing at Grandwest.

Coloured girls, sometimes
Glock pistols in a Gucci bag.

Coloured girls
won't count the cost
of loving you
hoping that you're true
while knowing that you are not.

Coloured girls
the uncrowned ache
of their mothers' dreams
sometimes broken
and while not shatterproof
are far more beautiful
than they care to know
and infinitely precious
much more than what we deserve.

Anybody who self-identifies as "coloured" in terms of the experiences detailed here, you are included here. I am using the clichés of coloured markers such as Wembley and the Plain but y'all from Phoenix and Wenties, New Brighton, Orlando. Mamelodi ... feel at home with what is laid down here. As Jose Marti, the Cuban patriot, said in his time, "There is only one Motherland and that is the human race."

An Elegy for Khwezi

Khwezi
a star ever-constant
over all homelands of truth
your moment in measured time is secured.

Quietly you embraced the immensity
infinitely beyond the Large Magellanic Cloud
of eternity after you came home

from Amsterdam as from Mbabane
as from homesteads deep in the valleys
of your unfathomable sorrow.

You spoke to us even when we would not listen:
"I may never be free from the agony of your treachery
but will forever cherish the freedom to speak
that my father got murdered fighting for."

Your testimony shamed us for entrusting
the shield of the nation to the premeditating
violator of your trust and of truth.

The spear of your poem, *"I am Khanga"*
held high in the clenched hope
of your warrior-spirit
sang of your unpretentious wisdom
treasuring the textured essence
of our shared memories of Africa.

The *khanga* adorns the bodies of women
bent over tea plants, green and fragrant
in Kenya's Limuru highlands
on the eastern rim of the Great Rift Valley.

A bright wrap of love binding mothers and babies
resting in the shade of awnings in Stone Town in Zanzibar.
"the perfect gift," you wrote, *"for new bride and new mother
alike."*

The seed of proverbs and poetry. A marker of history.
A celebratory testament to the imagination

This egalitarian fabric, your nightdress
on that night of silence and lies
led you back along the sad lanes of your unending exile.

Khwezi
ever-constant over all homelands of truth
your tender moment in our lives and measured time
is secured on the horns of our gratitude for releasing us
from the silence which betrayed you and ourselves.

Beyond the Night

for Lilian Masediba Ngoyi

You gave your all, when mournful clouds
shadowed a prodigious hope.

When salt was scarce and men
bowed their heads to the silence of might
you were a joyous clarion, a rising flame.

You surrendered your tender-green days
to our future and on an August day in that northern
wintered city – you and 20 000 front-line women

scythed us free of the amnesia
that muted the witness of our warrior days
and in the silence before the song
Strijdom fled from the petitions in your seamstress hands.

Now as we remember how 20 000 singing hearts
love-songed their lives to the bounded and forgotten
we wonder on this day at your prophecy Ma Lilian,

of how"*There has never been an age
that did not applaud the past
and lament the present*"
and at how soon it came to pass.

#SAMarch4Gaza: A Prayer

O most-loving Creator, we thank you for that day of 9 August 1956
and the women who marched on Pretoria, for their fierce
and audacious protest against the Pass Laws.
 We stand in gratitude for their witness and challenge
encouraging us as we march for Gaza
for streets of peace and homes with unlocked doors
and cups of cardamom-coffee on tables of friendship.
 We raise the flag of revolutionary hope and resolve
to the memory of Ma Lilian Ngoyi, Helen Joseph
Rahima Moosa,Ma Albertina Sisulu and Sophie Williams:
who led the way and we re-embrace their song:
'Wathinti Abafazi, wathint'imbokodo!'
 Let Benjamin Netanyahu and those who walk on his path
know this day that if 'You Strike a Woman, you Strike A Rock':
'Wathinti' mbokodo uzokufa!'
O God of surprises: Keen our spirits to the sound of your name.
Let it thunder in the dark, hidden caves of the heart
and of the souls of narrow, self-interest
where terror and hatred are spawned.
 And your song of justice and your will of freedom for all:
May it be for everybody –
for the Muslim child and the Jewish mother;
for Christian and Hindu and for those
of a diversity of creeds and belief.
And those who grapple this day to believe.
 Then bring us all to that place made holy by your love
- that shade of peace, the glory of your heaven
blessed for all who are wonderfully made in your image.
Amen

Soldier of Tambo

for Zelda

May the God of Biko and Krotoa
bless you with laughter
wrap you in a *tjalie* of courage
and fill you with peace
when harsh winds damn
the scent of buchu from your place.

Seek out quiet times
like the evening shades of Elim
and remember, *Morawiese kend*
that you are hewn from ancient rock.

Remember the *Groot Mense*
who danced the *koor-dans*
'til the dust covered the blood
on the bloodied soil of defeat
that they breathe in you.

Comrade, the stove is cold
pots are empty
and promises are brim-filled
with fat-bellied deception.
Songs of revolution are heard again.

The black, green and gold will always be ours
beyond this pause in a moment of history
because of ones such as you.

Sathima sang

for Daniel Yon

Sathima
because Duke asked
sang 'Solitude'.

She sang from a broken heart
which no one, she said, could really ever break
what the law of the land and a lover's lies
had not already broken.

Almost completely.
If not for the memory
of what she and her momma
and all the ones before knew
in their longing sadness of what was
beyond the mountain and Daniel's island
in the far distance of the ocean of the surging sea

that brought her home through the aching blues
brought her home in the raggedy roar
and rhythmed dip and dive
brought her home
like the laughter of lifting thighs
and bosomed cries

in the indigo dark of jazz
which brought her home
wherever she was and lived
brought her home

to Africa
of remembered names
and evasive dreams.

Africa of birdsong
heard in the shade of trees
along which the Camissa flowed
an *adagio* tempoed sigh of home.
Africa.

Lenten ash

I wrote a poem
about a woman.
She was beautiful

and she moved me
to write about her
while not knowing

what she looked like
where she lived.

Then I saw you
whose beauty
I could not name.

I tore the poem
into little pieces.

It fell softly
like Lenten ash
to the ground.

A letter to my father

Whether I called you 'dad' or 'daddy' I do not know.
I do not remember, ever, your voice say my name.

But I remember waiting, on a Saturday
there where you worked
at Nite-kem laboratory on Darling Street
for us to walk up Strand Street
across the Buitengracht onto Somerset Road
past Ebenezer near where we once lived
on Amsterdam Street.

Then watching, you, goal-keeper for Burnsdale your team
on Greenpoint Common. My sadness at the sight
of your mortality: stud-marked bruises on your dark skin.

I was seven when the divorce separated us.
All memories slip into forgetting.

Then one day, ten years later
when coming home after school
I found mum waiting at the front gate:
"Your father is very ill".

I was unable to associate myself with you
Until after the quiet train-ride
up the incline to Groote Schuur

we walked out of the lift on the floor of your ward
and the nurse told us that you had died.

The relief that I need not face the fear
of not recognising you.
My father. The guilt came soon.

It stayed long into my angry years.
My sullen, mute protest
against the neglected distance
when you were as close as Kensington to Elsies.

And the night at Koinonia
as the mist lay low
in the Valley of a Thousand Hills,
awakening from a tear-wet dream by a voice that said
"I am the father of the fatherless".

I wrote to my mother. I had forgiven you.
She need not worry about me.
The anger was less deep. I became a father.

Then on a day, mum
attending a funeral at Maitland Cemetery
walked over to your grave at Gate 10, knelt
took sand from your grave
placed it in her grandchild's hand and said,
"Stanley this is Michael's daughter.
Chiara, this is your grandpa."

I thanked her when she told me. Later, over tea.

Steve Bantu Biko said

Abafundisi
when you preach
on a Sunday
about our Friday
and Saturday night sins

don't be silent
about the sin
of allowing ourselves

to be oppressed and exploited
on all other God-given days of a week.

When the Hills Were Dark

On a morning such as this
when the hills were dark
with the colour of burnt grass
and the sun in the wind
was soft upon the land.

And the streets of the places
where we live
were quiet.

On a morning such as this
when the hills were dark
when not even you mother knew
you left us.

On my way from a conference in Soweto in 1980 I stopped over at the home of Mzi Mbangula's mother. He was a friend who lived in Zwelethemba, Worcester. When we met Ma Mbangula, her first question was "Where is my child?" That moment unlocked this poem

A drive-by question in two movements

Part I

We began to breathe. To organize our dreams in workshops
and winter schools at Dora Falcke.

Mountain hikes, to be guerrilla-fit - Greyton to McGregor.
In the sand dunes of Muizenberg over swigs of Old Brown
we hinted that we had read, *What is to be done*. Every word
we lied.

Part II

We were driving one night, late
From Westridge past Manenburg
from where Basil wouldn't leave for New York.

Vernie was singing, '*Venceremos*'
when Mzi posed the question
"What will we do with these buildings"
pointing to the flats, "after the revolution?"

I remember only his question
how it stunned me that there
could be a time after Apartheid.

A time beyond struggle
A revolutionary time.

When all will be free and when we
would visit your grave, Mzi, with our answers.

One Love

In 1982 I met Lincoln van Sluytman, a fellow from Guyana, in New York

Comrade, my brother, it's a long way from Georgetown
Guyana and New York to where I am, walking down
Raglin Road in Grahamstown, South Africa
longing to see you as I did on West 131st Street
telling me about Brother Malcolm. Masekela's horn
and Abdullah's Cape-scapes contouring the night.

And your smile, wide and rude-boy happy
like a clenched heart beating in the anthem we sang
in the Marcus Garvey Park in Harlem: "O se boloke sechaba!".
And you laughed at me, African and part of you
and Asia and the whole damn
wide world we breathe in word and being
from an African dawn to our western decline.

And laugh, my brother, for fighters
do not fear the despot's wrath
and laugh my brother
a part of me and the fist
that will sweep in the day
and may it soon come
when the people declare
from the Antilles to Angola
from Beirut to Brixton
from our lives to the heart of God
"Enough".

Yesterday

One night in 1983, during my second year of seminary, we had a debate about this or that.

Yesterday

someone smiled,

"thank you for what you said"

clasping my hand

my heart

in a hold of understanding.

Yesterday

someone

became a friend

asking about the tomorrow

that we build today.

Yesterday

I turned my face to the dark
and cried.

Padkos coloured by history

We were black enough to earn enough to splurge
on a feast of green-bean bredies: Sunday heaven
in a mystery of cloves and peppercorns.
Pot-roast beef. *Mngqusho* on the side.
Turmeric-yellowed rice and later
A choice of the cardamom scent in a bowl
of sago, or of jelly and custard.

The happy certainty on Monday of leftover lamb
On baked bread, red with beetroot salad
or the belly-comfort of *pens-en-pootjies*
curried silt in a history of run-aways
to the walk-aways at Aunty Meisie's
fiftieth wedding anniversary biduur

where it was so well with our souls
that we never gave thought to who we were
in the lull of the *skuins lê*
between the long, late lunch and afternoon tea
the heavy chain of time, dragging through
the thickening concrete of last night's *babalaas*

knowing, from the calm of a storm-blue Indian Ocean
that we were coloured like blood on the gallows steps
named in the song of church bells
refrained in the ache of the *athaan*
remembered like barakaat at Eid and *kifyaat kos*
in the sweetness of *gedatmelk*
as a saffron-sun slips over Signal Hill.

Mixed Blood

My blood is mixed
mixed with love and kindness
there in your voice
mixed with the salt
in the tears of our laughter.

My blood is mixed
mixed with every truth I lied
to get through a roadblock
or to cross a border of another day
in a winter of struggle.

My blood is mixed
mixed with the beat
throbbing in the heart of the word
proclaiming that God
took seven days to make a world
but taking His time

a lifetime
making the mixed-blood
you and me
thus ensuring that
there will always be music
in a world without end.

The autumn of Love

I knocked on the door
of your house in Mitchells Plain
in the last week of January 1980.

    I was bringing a letter
    from a friend of your sister.

You opened the door
my back was turned as I
secured my size-28, postman's bicycle
with a chain to the tar-pole of the car-port of the house.

    I turned at the sound of your soft laughter
    at me. At my bike of antiquity.

You were also amused
by my *ou ballie* fisherman's haversack
full of emptiness except for a diary, an apple
and a hard-covered collection of John Milton's poetry.

    A year later I wrote you this poem ...

        In the
            withering
                of a leaf
        in the fading
            of the day
                I love you.

(The poem was accompanied by a leaf as green as our young love)

On our wedding day

At Christ the Mediator in Mitchell's Plain
not far from where the UDF
was launched the year before
and Father Karl once fell asleep
on Archbishop Phillip Russell's shoulder

here, on our wedding day
Belinda played Abdullah's song
on a slightly out-of-tune piano.
We sang *'Sikelela iAfrika'* as the closing hymn.

And my mother looked
at my handcrafted
Greenwich Village bought
leather brogues and thought
of loaves of soft brown bread.

September child

Chiara, our first-born who saw the light of this life in September 1986

September child
embracing enemy territory
sometime
between
dark and dawn.

Nomalanga
our golden flower
in darkening days.

Jazz, your lullaby.
Freedom, your morning prayer
and Africa, our gift to you.

Promise child
of what we
may never know.

We bow
to the wisdom
of your generous smile

warm and spilling
from
the home
of original innocence.

So Much to Declare

Entering South Africa in 1982 after a visit to the UK.

London, a frozen, dark distance
from sunny skies over Joburg
as BA flight 307 touches ground on my anxious land.

Yet rejoice, O my soul!

AJ Luthuli International Airport where the open doors
of peace and friendship welcomes all who love freedom
and our people to a liberated South Africa.

Blue eyes, warm beneath the peaked cap of officialdom
admire the miniature bust of VI Lenin
COLLETS price tag still intact.

Porters on lunch-time break grin Amandla smiles.
Mbaqanga happiness fills the excited queue.

I wonder how the debate about a new name for our country
was faring and Phila's suggestion that the Settlers Monument
in Rhini, once Grahamstown, be made into the biggest beer-hall
in the Eastern Cape.

And last year, like a dream, walking with Fidel Castro
Along Bernard Fortuin Avenue past the Alex la Guma Cultural
Centre in Elsies River where the Orient Bioscope used to be
and the *Commandante* laughing through his beard at my account
of how we youngsters used to cheer when Zorro rode onto the
screen and into our lives.

And Daniel, yes Ortega, saying that they did the same when he
was a boy in Managua and Che somewhere in jungled Bolivia.

"*Anything to declare?*"
Voice hard like blue eyes hard
like rock tumbling down
crashing ten-storeys down
dangling like time.

"*Anything to declare?*"
Blue eyes shouting, "*Ja, koolie-boesman*
with your wing-tip shoes
button-down collar and new blue suit.
This is South Africa!"

Anything to declare?"
whipping up the Riotous Assembly
of my fear.

"*Yes*", I smile from the tip of my trembling toes,
"*South Africa belongs to all, and to me and you, Piet*"

He does not hear the roar of "Mayibuye!" at Freedom Square.
"The People Shall Govern" I assure him, speaking now
with the voice of the thousands who gathered
at the Congress of the People.

"*Goed. You may go.*"
I pick up my suitcase and my ruffled courage
and walk past security, past the soldiers.

My Mandela t-shirt
sweat-wet against my beating heart...

Ocean View

for Gladys and Beverley, for Peter and Albert and Donald.
And Martha. For everyone

On 21 July 1985, President PW Botha declared a national State of
Emergency. As a mark of protest many people across South Africa
lit candles as signs of hope, and stood, often in silence, outside
their homes. Some placed their candles on the windowsills of their
darkened homes in the evenings.

Tomorrow we leave this place.
the car overloaded and with heavy hearts
we cross the mountains of lead.
　　Tomorrow we leave this valley of solitude
where at night the sea-breeze blows soft
along untarred roads, past fear-locked houses
where nostalgia and regret embrace.
　　But tonight
tonight we are here
with a candle in the doorway
without fear of the dark and the devil in the moon.
　　Because even here, here in this place
where the sun also shines
here too
　　we fight the monster that murders
our children and bedevils our days.
　　Here in the name of the Lord
We will crush and destroy it
so that the beginning of the day
wherein the lion and the lamb
will dwell together
will be hastened.

The land is dark

The land is dark
and the fog
drifts off the False Bay waters.

Wet, heavy dew
a crystal halo
on the lamp lights
along Hazeldene Avenue.

The dogs are let loose into the night

I know they come
my love.
Before their shadows
crowd our room
say my name. Hold me.

And when I'm gone
and dark lies the land

then sing
sing the anthem low
and weep
my love.

Flight of the Spear

On 1 June 1981 ANC guerrillas sabotaged strategic petroleum facilities.
These included four reservoirs at the SASOL 1 oil-from-coal plant

When SASOL burnt
the streets of the townships
danced to the rhythm of freedom songs.
Constantia was as quiet as the grave.

      When SASOL burnt
      Houghton waited
on the trigger of a gun.

In the train next morning Bafana shouted
"Hamba kahle, Umkhonto we Sizwe!"
We laughed our agreement.

The 'Whites Only' side sat tight-lipped
behind their newspapers
when SASOL burnt.

How Come?

I wake up on this day of OR's birthday
a postmodern Rip van Winkle
wondering how come
I didn't get the memo that said
that the Freedom Charter
was only revolutionary poetry
a romantic phase; a potion imbibed
by fevered youth born for martyrdom
compelled onto a road
to do what must be done
to fulfil history's mandate
of a working-class

freed from the shame of poverty
and the fear of the power
of organized capital.

When we stepped
Cape Flats *tekere* into the marching vanguard
of woman, the worker, of Soweto youth
opening the road to this future
beyond bullets and charred dreams.

Tambo, we heed your caution about the wedge-driver
of the thieves who grow rich on the back of our victory.
Tambo, *lithle izulu*: we hear your call
from the heaven of Sandino, of Luthuli
and of Malcolm and Martin
of Lilian and Helen: "... *usafundisa 'majoni* ..."
when freedom still ain't free ...

Like Langston

Oom Reg September, 3 June 1923 – 22 November 2013

I never knew you wrote poetry
distilling love in lines of languid longing
like Langston and Neruda, like Mongane Serote.

I never knew of, but can only imagine
your yearning for brisk sea-soaked days
like those you knew

when you stood on the rocks
near Kalk Bay harbour
baiting the hook, gutting the catch

guided by the sonorous laughing voice
of the father whom you adored.

All this of memory's gathering
like the mist-soft
seven days rain of a Cape winter.

And you, hunkered in the homestead
shaded 'neath banana and mango groves
the moon full and yellow above Dar-es-salaam

dreaming of places and loved ones
the touch and sigh
of a promised revolution.

When Madiba visited Ashton

*After the release of Madiba folk who had felt the brunt of unbridled
racism took to the streets, embarked on consumer boycotts and general
acts of civil disobedience.*

I remember that day in Zolani-Ashton
when you blessed a hall with your name.
I wasn't there. The ones who were
recall your regal grace, your Madala sexiness
as you stood there beneath the scalding Boland sun
the Langeberg Mountains dull-grey and curious
behind you.

They talked about the warmth
in your eyes and your declared
pride in them and their unsung bravery.

Now as I await the tears still to come
from somewhere close but deep
in the hidden mystery of my soul.

I wish I had been there and had obeyed
the call to break my cathedral-based fast
for freedom and an end to police violence

to join all on that day when a Prince of Men
stood handshake and hug-close
to annoint Ma Memani with a lifetime of joy
which not even the poverty of these times
could ever take away.

Just outside Ashton

I buried the Makarov and
a stash of Kalashnikov bullets
at the edge of a field of aloes

forty metres northeast of a tree
on the last bend before Ashton.
Just in case, my comrade said.

They widened the road
When Madiba came by
on his walk to freedom.

The tree is gone.

I have a bottle of merlot
from the wine estate
where aloes grow

near where a tree once stood
on a Boland wine route.

I keep it corked
for my comrade.

Just in case he loses
the taste
for single malt.

A Poet's life

for Oom Don Mattera

This is not a poem yet
but only the first touch of intention
but when I saw you, quiet, unnoticed
at the edge of the busy crowd
    I, without a thought of decorum and place
knelt, kissed and held your hand
and we spoke as if we had met before
    and I felt the way I did when I first read
Azanian love song
and knew then that another knew
what it means to be a *bushie wat ken.*
    And so I salute you, Mattera, poet of all the people
Want ek notch djy's 'n jieta wat wiet warrie buchu blom.
    And when you declared our love for Madiba
I wanted to call out to you there
on that distant stage
not to say a word
not a sound of a syllable more
    just to stand there and let us see you
the poet-prophet who sang out of the heart of the brave
of a time 'when freedom finally walks the land.'
    But this is not a poem yet
only the slight stutter of gratitude
for a poet's life.

Biko

Born of Mathew and Alice Mamcete
brother to Bukelwa and Khaya
and Nobandile, the lastborn.

Death ambushed you on the road of your own *Via Dolorosa*.
The way of suffering beyond Nongqawuse's place of sorrow
to where the surplus-city Dimbaza uncovered the secrets of evil.

And on a good day you danced like a Joburg *kleva*
from Ginsberg to Keiskammahoek
and every place in-between

to where, finally
the handcuffs of Pretoria bound you
at a place just beyond Makana's Kop.

Biko, our forever young
our courage when prophets
sought shelter in mansions of silence
our pride when the dirt of propaganda kissed deception
bowing our heads under the weight of shame.

Biko, they killed your body. And we wept at the sight
of your dark, bruised and beaten beauty.

And now all over this forsaken Azania
you, like resurrection hymns
like the promise of empty graves
like the sound of the marching poor
you come singing our forgotten songs.

Now Is Not the Time

said Mandela

for the Church to seek
the cosiness of the sanctuary
while arriving late at the empty tomb of truth

as the *Corpus Christi,* the children of our martyrs
and the duped disciples of a franchised faith
of the gospel of avarice

are burdened by the shame of a nation
that will not feed and shelter its own
promenading jack-booted brutality

when they, the people, seek a better life
beyond the quinquennial promise of the ballot
when they are citizens for that day

that blesses their chosen
to lead them.
Nowhere.

Now, in these days of commissioned truth
and retracting reconciliation

proclaim insurrection
share kindness and food
and clothe yourself daily
with commitment to be
the all-embracing arms of God.

Uncoupling

He knew in the certainty of his silence
that she was akin to a treasure
hidden like in a field of Strelitzia abloom
in an outrage of blues and yellows.

What was there not to love?
Her wide grinned smile
her lilt of voice
her eye-squinting laugh

and her spirit that sought no caution
birthed, as it was
in a season of flowering anger.

The arsenal of patriarchal custom
fluttered in its futile flight.
He deployed the functional poetry of flowers
strewing it along the path to her impudent heart.

Her arms surrendered to the sigh of love
embraced the years that blessed
and then uncoupled

the longing certainty
of uncovering a treasure
hidden in a field.

Leaving

How can I miss you
when you never leave?
you once told me.

Your laugh
the silver in the cloud
of our parting.

And still I pack and board planes
that soar above deserts
and savannas in the dark below.

And sit, like now
outside a cafe
on Helsinki's *Kaisaniemenkatu*

listening to passing trams
and bicycles and lovers sing
the syllabled softness of your name

as I look to see you
maybe turn the corner of my heart
to where I wait.
Not missing you at all.

Eina

for Diana Ferrus

A two-syllable knock
on the door that opens
to where we live
down the road from yesterday

seeing the dawn light
on Tradouw
the elands trail

guiding us to healing pastures
distant from the place
where we danced

beneath the fullness
of the blue
dark moon

singing a song
a prayer
a sigh beyond words.

I like my coffee

black and bitter
like the sistas
who wouldn't read
the poems I never sent.

Who saw the *clevas*
The Florsheim *jietas* from Eldos.
And not me.

I like my coffee
percolated and amber brown
filling me to the brim of contentment

like you do
long after the mug
is empty
and cold.

If I was in Cuba today

for Blanche la Guma

If I was in Cuba today you would find me at the
Cementerio de Cristóbal Colón at the grave of Alex la Guma
our District Six Dostoevsky.

I will sing: "*da ga'rie padtjie narie kramat toe*".
A coconut shell slanging a *goema riddim*.
You will catch the tune and sing with me
as I libate the ground with a tot of buchu brandy

cigar smoke infused with a sniff of Jamaican sunshine
the non-majat, forgotten familiar of home.

If I was in Cuba today we will slow salsa under a Carib moon
keening low, like old lovers do.

We will sing about, "*jou matras en my kombers*"
like Blanche and Alex would once have sung
their eyes on the waters of the *Playas del Este*
their hearts blissed by the wind

breezing down the moonlit lanes beyond Roger Street
across the Parade to the bay of their sighed longing.

I will stand in gratitude at your grave, Uncle Alex
in Havana today, and to say that we have not forgotten
you and your words that led us through the fog
and beyond the night of draconian ghosts
to where we walk the days of freedom.

Wealth

He got drunk
on wine
he could not afford.

Satiated on a meal
someone else paid for

he walked home
to where
Coltrane

made him feel
like he owned
the world.

Where the river flows

for Eugene Skeef. For our martyrs, remembered and those neglected in memory.

I will be there where the river flows, my brother
like hope that wells from dreams in laughing days
before pain was memory and love its healing
scar-touched balm.

I will be there with all my heart, my brother
looking on from the burning hills of our wintered land
waiting for the promised rain.

I will be there when your words, my brother
like herb-scented water, bathe the wounds
of the dead who cannot die while bullets mark
the roads to the graves of the fallen of Colenso, Tembisa,
Alexandra and Belville's taxi-ranks.

Let us gather at the river, my brother
along with the dead who cannot die
while the mouths that informed, who named the path
the *cul-de-sac* of our betrayed ones
still name us as their own, the kith and kin of struggle.

We will meet them, the shepherds who sing
who sing of freedom, the fat of the slaughtered lamb
glistening on their faces once hidden in the dark
but now lit by the moon, bright and blue in the river.

Let us gather there, my brother
where our martyrs will lead us
in the dance of the resurrected.

Thanayi

Bra Zinga notch

By the time I turned into Queen Victoria Street
Stimela was playing on the radio and uncried tears
self-summoned from every sad homeland of banished hope
surrendered to the defeat of regret, flooded my eyes
as I drove along Bo-Kaap's Rose Street.

I don't know about his mistakes, preached Oom Don
But it's never wrong to love a woman. Never, never.
And from the deep well of experience, he declared,
Especially when that woman loves you back.

Ain't that a fact. Open the door of your heart,
ma se kinners. See how love stepped over
the threshold of your life.

How you welcomed her with tender respect
like we did when love stormed through our hearts
like a Soviet T-26 flame-throwing tank
and *moered* us all over freedom park.

I didn't mean to hurt you, she smiled.
I just want to free you.

From our innocence, our trusting nature?
Los daai ding, Groot Man, Bra Zinga, was told
in the dark days of Sophiatown, by a Little Jesus
who in life made the misery less so
and whose music sounds even more beautiful.
now that he's gone.

Brutus, Siempre

for Dennis Brutus

Between Christmas and Epiphany
a great tree fell, unheard
in the silent African night
his fleeting spirit within sighting sigh
of cloud-shrouded Table Mountain.

Between the Island of Makana
and the receding shoreline of freedom
this bearded colossus from eBhayi

referenced from the archives of injustice
the simple truths, the Magnificat of freedom
now footnoted into the his-stories of boardrooms

and the like from whence capitalism's newly-ordained
baptised him ultra-left.

Between this now and a past of commemoration services
the Caspirs idling promise of the violence to come
in a church hall in Mitchell's Plain, a chorus of young voices:
        Today in prison, they will sing just one song
sourcing an elusive courage,
        ... strong and steady...
numbering themselves amongst those
        ... who will do the much that needs be done ...

Brutus is, as he was then, a muse of freedom.

Between Christmas and Epiphany this magus of the poors
paused. His ears alert to children's voices on old Hanover Street
detailed between the banjo chord
and Boeta Achmat's *goema*-steady, tenor saxophone
    ... da korrie Alabama ...

And then a slow, resolute turning towards
the orange-hued sun imbuing
the Hottentots Holland Mountains

his African-Latino-Palestinian soul
blazing a path on his march
onto other geographies of freedom ...

Siempre, siempre!

You will never die

Nomzamo Winnie Madikizela-Mandela passed away on Easter Monday 2 April 2018.

Mama Winnie, Apostle of freedom, you will never die.
Risen, as you were, in Trayvon Martin
shot and killed in Sanford, Florida, USA.

You will never die. Defiant. Resolute like Ahed Tamimi
unsettled and terrorised in the West Bank. You will never die.

Your spirit rose loud
in the silent anti-rape protest
of four young women
fearless in their flouting
of customary deference to the posture of protocol.

You will never die
Nomzamo Winnie Madikizela-Mandela.
Rouse the fallen. Your stoic witness summons us
to the frontline of the abandoned barricades

where you live in those who find no value
in the currency of surrender. You will never die.
> *A woman soldier shouted:*
> *Is that you again? Didn't I kill you?*
> *I said: You killed me ... and I forgot, like you, to die.*
> (from *Jerusalem* by Mahmoud Darwish)

Alchemy

Nina sang
and
the sun

felt
like
love on my skin.

In the name of all

"You Ain't Gonna Know Me, 'Cos You Think You Know Me"
Mongezi Feza

Think again, when you look at me
masala-hued, ebony dark or
all peaches and cream and then dare decree
He's not an African.

       Think of your myth about my easy road to freedom
       defined by my *rol*, my loose-limbed, raucous *jiet*
       in the New Year's carnival of the city
       where I was loved into being.

Think again when you write my story and edit my essence
as a footnote in a chapter of the book of Apartheid.
       Listen, when you hear the lilt of my patois
       as I answer to Mariam, Fransiena or Shawn
       and then sneer or sympathise, *they have no culture.*

Have you seen me praise-dance on laughing, Sunday streets
or in the green shade of the sad trees at Gate 9
at Maitland Cemetery?

       Think of this, when ensconced in your West-coast cottage
       snuggled in the fire-logged warmth of a weekend retreat
       on the lower slopes of the Langeberg.

       Or, when gazing down on the bejewelled beauty
       of the bay from the Cape-Quartered heights
       of Loader Street that once was my home:

that I am of the first stewards of this southern distance.
I am of those who danced a worship-stirred step
on the slopes of the Hoerikamma
blessed in the light of the new moon.

      I am the unsung *mkhonto* who raised spear
      without caution, against the Viceroy de Almeida
      and his marauding marines.

My body, a shield for my children, flesh of my flesh
and of my colonial-martyred bones.

And when you see me marooned
on the water-logged Cape Flats
in Manenberg and in Langa, Bokmakierie and Nyanga
garrisoned by poverty and the lies of history, then

      then, listen in the dark of dawn for the voice
      that calls you to yourself. It sings of the greatness
      of God and of the truth that all land
      and all people are not to be owned
      that the goodness of the earth is to be shared
      as a sign and measure of God's love.

Maybe then, if you fall to your knees in gratitude
for a truth about your acquisition of my enslaved flesh
and labour indentured to your prosperity

      you may learn something of the African you are.
      And then, may your thoughts
      guide you home to a new beginning.

For the beauty of it all

On bent knee
we show love of self and of others.
On bent knee
we recast the Cross of Calvary
in how Black Lives Matter.

Here we witness to the greatness of love
seeding our faith at the barricades
of justice for all
for the black and brown
la Raza of the world.

Here the mustard-like seed of love
powers the world being born
from the terror and the shame of history.

A world groaning
breaking forth from the Struggle
to Breathe
to love unfettered
to live the fulfilment
of God's longing for heaven on earth.

Here we bend the knee of our heart
with the LGBTQ+ community
and out of love for all God's children denied,
in whatever way, the fullness of the beauty of life.

Here we rise, Beloved
unshackling the weight of history.

This poem

This poem
alive
with a life-long
curiosity

ponders
how the sword
in your hand

shaped
the cross
on which you killed

your god who died
for me.

Uncle Kathy

Ahmed Kathrada: 1929 - 2017

Tender love has been your shield
and courage your apron of servanthood.
Your soul, once awash with longing
For comrades who shared with you
the frugal feasts of your island fort
now rest unburdened of the weight of care
that led you to the certainty of prison.
You returned to the streets of struggle
in the spring of our revolution
your heart embalmed with the will
and strength of the Almighty.
With a mystic's grace you embraced
the shaming contradictions of unfulfilled promises
and pursued the discipleship of mind and body
undeterred by the clamour of glory and the lure
of the Sabbath of the veteran.
Sweet, gentle brother of the people
you leave us, strengthened by your kindness
your fearless reprimand of the soul self-evictees.
Those led by the morally blind.
Rest in the certainty that you leave us
beatified by your exemplary witness
as we gather unbowed, against the merchants of greed
in this season of reckoning and gathered resolve.

The naming of things

Let us live on streets named after trees
in towns and cities known by its flowers
and the laughter of children
like Camissa, our place of sweet waters,
known as it was since the days of our ancients.

Jacaranda blossoms and baobabs pleasure
without deference to protocols observed.

The integrity of the aloe and the sycamore fig tree
stand beyond all reproach. Luxurious pin-cushioned
proteas and the whistling thorn tree
elicit no cause of concern of illegal gain.

We fear no assault from solitary clivias
as the solemn mopane maintain
a delicate, peaceful decorum.

The Serengeti and the Gariep
won't overwhelm you with doubt
about your choice at the ballot box

and the acacia will still shade you regardless
of your view on the environment or against
which name you made your mark.

The proud marula and vygies in pinkly purples
won't betray or stab you in the back
and the non-sectarian oak
and the arum lily are tendency free.

Let us live, in our unnamed Mzantsi republic
like trees with its sheltering shade
and flowers with its beauty
not seeking nor expecting any gain but for
the joy of the sun and the moon of our days.

Singing, we rise

On 28 August 1985, thousands of marchers set off from Athlone, Cape Town to Pollsmoor Prison to demand the release of Nelson Mandela.

Four thousand en route to Pollsmoor. Four thousand marching
and singing, walking with banners and laugher and empty hands.
Two minutes to disperse. It takes two minutes
to unfurl the banner that reads: *A nation that loves martyrdom
shall never be enslaved.*

Two minutes to disperse. Four thousand who had walked
a lifetime's distance from freedom, kneel in the road.
A tired elephant in the heat of the day.

Two minutes since when? Since Sharpeville '61
when came 'a time to resist and fight?'

Two minutes past the day when Kathrada
Mbeki, Sisulu, Mandela and the many
were herded into their Island cage.

Two minutes past the dawn
when the poet Benjamin Moloise
was hung, his 'one solitary life' defiant
in the cruel Pretoria dawn.

Let us pray.
> Above, the unhappy rattle of a helicopter.
> Ahead, the restrained blue hounds of terror
> gun-proud, bullet-crazy. Give the Hotnots hell.
> (Lord, let me not be a coward).

Then, the lone-lilting *Our Father*
and, as in a chapel along the way
who art in heaven
Singing, we rise to meet the enemy
hallowed be thy name.
(Fear is a place in the lungs where air can't reach*).*

Disperse and pursue. Grab and tear apart:
thy kingdom come on earth.
Break bones. Thrash your hate across the breasts of a child
not unlike your own: *as in heaven.*

Oh, my God! The blood on their hands.
The blood of Abel slain again and again.
As in the beginning.

And, in the roar of their madness,
The dogs of dread laugh in the face
of our bloodied anger.

And Malusi's voice, ragged and thin with questioning:
The Lord is here.
And our voices, loud with the joy of the saints:
His Spirit is with us.

On the ground, amidst the wreckage of peaceful protest
the face of the young Mandela
calm and resolute.

Your hands

for our Arch

Your hands
cradling hope
hung black

against the hard sky
that was never blue for us.

The sun shone for others.
You giggled. Your laughter
a choir of naughty angels.

The cold rain felt good.
The fierce wind became a friend.

God, you said, your voice
a moon of rising incredulity, *knew us*.
We were loveable because He loved us.

We were not forgotten. Our pain made God cry.
God was with us, even when we felt He was not.

Your hands, beautiful like God's
unclenched, bless the sheet of your bed.

The Blue Sky

for those who did nothing; for those who gave everything

The tree I planted
with fervid seeds
provides no shade for my children.

The house I built on
the ruins of hope
stands empty.

And you whom I loved
and who loved me
with a yearning heart

now look beyond
my outstretched hand
and see only the eyes of the stranger
who scorned

the promise of the tree
the dreams of our longing
the work of our day
and our simple faith
in the blessing of the blue sky.

Kyle's piano

notes
me over
steaming savannah's
to Nordic fiords
where I sip

lemon and ginger tea
from a green
banana leaf

my visa
with my clothes
at home.

Camissa of the clandestine

for Zenzile KhoiSan

The jacaranda tree, aflush with lilac, guards the old building
Church House on Queen Victoria Street where we decoded
the gospel of evil proclaimed by the co-opted
the quislings of the kingdom of the demonic, still stands.

Now indifferent to the cold, soggy purple flowers fallen
like our drug-dulled children who recline night and day
against its walls seeking, inducing some respite
from the clamour on their soul-torn lives.

And somewhere, and I didn't know it then
deep below the ground
now covered with used condoms
and broken needles
the dead dreams of young lovers

artesian streams flow with certainty
towards the bay beyond
there where the statue of Jan van Riebeeck
cries out to be limpet-bombed
to smithereens. Like our dreams.

A Psalm of Solidarity

Thank God for the day when freedom
came home like love cascading
from the mountains of the moon
colouring the day in hues of saffron and blue
even at noontime.

And now they plot to drag your country
into the misery of the past.
The shadow of Somoza skulks in Honduras
the star-spangled beast plundered Grenada
intervenes in El Salvador

mad with the wine of debauchery
the global power whores of a reborn Babylon.

Have they forgotten Cuba
the graves of their children in Vietnam
how they crept out of Beirut?

Do they think that Maurice Bishop is dead
when Padre Romero never died?
When Carlos Fonseca is forever amongst us
like Solomon Mahlangu who lived to say
Tell my people that I love them.

Tomas Borge, Daisy Zamora, Ernesto Cardenal,
Nora Astorga, Monica Baltedano, Danilo Rosales.
The God of Gaspar Garcia Laviana and of our lives
who led you from the mountains.

Who stood amongst you at the barricades of Jinotepe
sheltered you in the safe houses of Managua, Leon
will not abandon you to the fate of the betrayer's kiss

and we, singing the songs that strengthen us
even and especially now, will pray with you
filled with a deep hope in you

as you live your lives for life
for the people who never surrender.

Jericho Walls

In memory of Neil Aggett: 6 October 1953 - 5 February 1982

*Manenberg is a housing area outside Cape Town located in the sand dunes
of the Cape Flats. It is an Apartheid-era gulag designated as a Coloured
Group Area in the 1960s. Basil 'Manenberg' Coetzee, renowned Cape Town
saxophonist, earned his nickname from his evocative rendition of the song
by that name which was composed by Abdullah Ibrahim. It was his raw,
soaring solo, evoking the bleak defiance aspect of township life, that
determined its place in the popular consciousness of the nineteen-eighties.
It was also the favourite party piece of Neil Aggett who died in detention at
the hands of the Special Branch. He was 28 years old. Writing from prison,
Oscar Mpetha, referred to Neil as 'a man of the people.' With this simple,
sparse phrase, weighted by the seeming incongruity of a white martyr of
privileged background, he adorned the memory of the fallen trade unionist
with the highest of praises. Neil was buried from St Mary's Anglican
Cathedral in Johannesburg. The funeral service was a blend of traditional
Anglican ritual and hymns, struggle songs of defiance, and the rhetoric of
revolution which underscored the anger of the largely black congregation of
mourners. 'Manenberg' was played during the funeral service.*

Die hang-gat sax

     roer die lahnies

         tot in hulle moer

             innie Joburg Cathedral.

*'And when the people heard the sound of the seven trumpets they
gave a mighty shout and Jericho's walls came tumbling down.'*
– The Book of Joshua 6 verse 20

O sistas of the land

and for all who were told julle hettie hare nie

Your hair is the crown of your gorgeous glory
the facts of the pain of your untold story
like when the *swirl-kous* crinkle cuts
unsmooths as the day goes *kaplats*.

And that afro, *hourit soe* honey-brown
Or Nama-blonde but wear your crown
as the Queen of Bontas, Princess of the Tjatjies

you're our earth, our wind and our galley fire
our First Ladies *onner 'n geliende* hair-dryer.

Your hair, like a ghetto-guerrilla
Never *skuiled* from a fight with the *dikding* southeaster
or the harsh sunlight:
      You just walked, rhythm to the side
      sassy in your stride
      'n vollende Flats cherrie
      your ego your pride, to the eye, rock-steady

When ferns fringes fall flat and frazzled
your look and glare checks you not at all rattled
and your hairs go *gemince en ongedo*

but still you roll like Maya Angelou.
And even when *gedoek* for the Wednesday *biduur*
when you *joebel en juig innie gees ennie gier*
Broer Jiggels will try not to stare
as he thanks God for the body
(okay, and for the bounce of your hair).

When I hugged you at the peace at Sunday Mass
in the row behind the late Leonard and a surly lass
there in your purdey style under the white *berêtjie*
I could smell how much dhanya there was in the curry for lunch.

Don't go changing the coloureds of your hair however *gedyes*:
be it *kroes*, curly or glads in a beehive high rise
let wella-straight go bankrot but neva eva compromise
on how the *Lahnie-van-Boe* made and A-graded you
as you grand parade in *pantoffels* or stiletto shoe.

You our lady soul and our shining star
so big respect for the loving
tjatjarag way *youse* are.

A Letter from Factreton, June 1986

for Trevor Manuel

Dear God
For a long while I believed that you were white
and doubted your love for colouring me brown.

In a candlelight halo, while the primus stove
spluttered in the corner of our room on Singh's yard
I said awkward prayers in my shamefaced patois.

Maybe you lived somewhere beyond
in a Camps Bay-like heaven
where ghetto prayers were not heard after dark.

Then Stokely said, *Black Power!*
And Steve refrained, *Amen, mfo.*
And Daphne, *I want my coffee black*
and light-eyed Trevor continued
and strong, like our people!
And a brother replied, *Damn white liberal.*

I haven't seen him for a while
him being the longest held detainee in the Western Cape.
As for these days, O mystery beyond words
it makes no difference what your colour is.
Your being Zulu-speaking is just fine enough for me.

The dance of falling stars

for Errol Dyers

My people
our poets are few.
Our warriors lie unnamed
unsung beneath the weight of rocks
and fynbos covered battlefields.

My people
Our goema griots sound our songs
known only by the stars
and the blood-soaked moons
that trace our tears, shades
our sighs of sadness as it keens
over the burial ground of lies
dug from the myths of history.

My people
ours is the promise
of the endless deserts
the dark clouds lush with rain
and the seeds of crushed wild fig trees.

Behold our beauty
my people, even
in the dance of falling stars.

Promise

The warm, soft light
shadows
a quiet longing

for friends
we won't see
for a while

beyond the ache
and dust
of memory.

Pandemic piety

...do not be anxious... - Philippians 4 verse 6

These days I think about death with more clarity. Until now I had always thought that I could take my time considering death as if it was optional: a choice that I could exercise in terms of timing when I would be laid to rest.

Now I lie awake longer and more often than usual, considering my options. There are times when without thought, I sing, *Hold me close, let Your love surround me* surrendering to the power of the Cape Flats funeral anthem: love leaning on every saddening note, the familiar rock to rest against. Now I lie awake, conscious of my co-morbidities and I plan my funeral no longer as a 'should I die' but rather as a 'when I die.' Priests and imams in their number will sing in the choir of the silent. A Bo-Kaap Tablighi followed by my family, will say a few words.

After the silence, long enough for the sound of tears to dry, a recording of Abdullah Ibrahim's *Blues for a Hip King* will be played. After the first bar, an unknown tenor saxophonist will step onto the Cathedral's red carpet covered dias. Her improvisation will cause many to wonder why they hadn't attended church more often. And the peace of God will rise forth and up from the depth of their unknown self. Joy will flood their souls in ways beyond all understanding, and laughter will shade their hearts. Henceforth, from that day on, that which they feared would be gone.

Glossary

I know where me from

familia:	family
goema drum:	a hand-held drum made from a small wooden wine barrel of which one end is covered with the skin of an animal. It is popularly associated with the traditional New Year's Carnival held in Cape Town.
I-and-I:	We. Often used in place of 'you and I' or 'we' among Rastafari to indicate the oneness and unity of people

#SAMarch4Gaza

Wathint' Abafazi, Wathint' Imbokodo'	Xhosa: You strike the women, you strike the rock. These words are generally associated with the Women's March to the Union Buildings on 9 August 1956 to protest against the pass laws under Apartheid.

Soldier of Tambo

tjalie	colloquial Afrikaans word for swaddling blanket
buchu	an aromatic plant indigenous to the Cape region, used for medicinal purposes. Botanical name: *agathosma betulina*
Morawiese kend	Moravian child; '*kend*' is a phonetic representation based on colloquial pronunciation of the Afrikaans word 'kind' meaning child
Groot Mense	Literally translated from Afrikaans it means 'big people / adults.' It is also used to refer to

71

'elders' which is the way that it is being used in this context.

koor-dans   praise dance. A form of worship that has its origins in the Pentecostal Churches of Southern Africa. It is no doubt influenced by the trance or healing dances of the indigenous San people.

Steve Bantu Biko said

Abafundisi: preachers

One Love

O se boloke sechaba save our nation (this is a line in the new South African anthem)

Padkos coloured by history

bredie: stew

umngqusho: a dish made of samp with sugar beans, onions and potatoes

pens-en-pootjies   tripe and trotters

skuins lê   literally translated it means 'to lie sideways'; used colloquially it means 'to take a nap'

babalaas   a hangover, taken from the Zulu word 'isibhabalazi'.

athaan   Islamic call to prayer

barakat   Arabic for blessing. Used customarily to refer to food or cakes given to guests to take home after a festive gathering.

Kifyaat kos   a basic meal of meat, carrots and peas served at the conclusion of a Muslim funeral

gedatmelk   a sweet, milky drink served at Muslim prayer meetings following a funeral

The autumn of love

Ou ballie   slang for old man and in this context, it is used to suggest old-fashioned mannerisms or style

On our wedding day

UDF   The mass-based United Democratic Front was a national movement which was launched in Mitchells Plain, Cape Town in August 1984.

So much to declare

koolie-boesman   Indian-bushman (derogatory)

A Poet's life

Bushie wat ken   Colloquial; a streetwise person of Khoekhoe descent

Eina

Eina   a word of Khoekhoe origin for 'ouch'

Flight of the Spear

Hamba kahle, Umkhonto we Sizwe   Go well, Spear of the Nation

How Come?

Cape Flats *tekere*   Cape Flats crazy

Lihle izulu   beautiful heaven in Xhosa

Usafundisa 'majoni   he still teaches' soldiers in Xhosa

A Poet's life

ek notch djy's 'n jieta wat weet wa' die buchu blom   Colloquial; I know that you are a hustler who knows where the *buchu* flowers

If I was in Cuba today

daga'rie padtjie narie kramat toe   Colloquial Afrikaans, meaning 'there is the road to shrine'

the non-majat   Colloquial; good quality

jou matras en my kombers   your mattress and my blanket

Thanayi

ma se kinners   Colloquial Afrikaans; mommas' children

moered	assaulted (slang)
Los daai ding	Leave it alone
Groot Man	Big Man

Brutus, Siempre

Poors	I came across the term in Ashwin Desai's, *The Poors* which highlights the "counter-identities" of communities struggling to live, to survive under abject and crowded living conditions in a post-apartheid South Africa. Referring to the residential flats of Chatsworth, a historical Indian township outside Durban on the country's east coast, Desai writes: "While it still had a certain resonance, it was silly to think of the area as "Indian." An increasing number of the flats were occupied by African tenants and, when the chips were down, everyone thought of themselves as a community, as *the poors"*.
Da korrie Alabama	Colloquial Afrikaans meaning 'here comes the Alabama.' It is often sung during the New Year Carnival in Cape Town and is a reference to the CSS Alabama, a US Confederate war ship. The Alabama was involved in expeditionary raids off the coast of Cape Town in 1863 during the American Civil War.

Jericho Walls

Die hang-gat sax	a ghetto-sounding saxophone; *hang-gat* is a colloquial use of the Afrikaans words for 'hanging backside', and its meaning is context-specific and would not be apparent from a direct translation.
roer die lahnies	moved the white people emotionally

tot in hulle moer	deeply moved; the word *moer* has several meanings, determined by context
innie Joburg Cathedral	in the Joburg Cathedral

O sistas of the land

Julle hettie hare nie	you don't have hair; used to mock someone who does not have 'good' (i.e. sleek) hair
swirl-kous	a night-bonnet made from nylon pantyhose used to keep hair straight while sleeping
kaplats	flat
hourit soe	keep it like that
Queen of Bontas	Queen of Bonteheuwel. This township on the Cape Flats was often abbreviated to *Bontas.*
Princess of the tjatjies	Princess of Manenberg. This township also on the Cape Flats was nicknamed *Tjatjies*
geliende	borrowed
never skuiled from a fight	never avoided a fight. *Skuil* is the Afrikaans word for 'hide' or 'seek shelter'
dik ding	Translated literally from Afrikaans it means 'thick thing'. Often used to refer to someone with a superior attitude, in this case, it refers to the notorious Cape south-Easter wind.
vollende	completely
gemince en ongedo	*mince* is the word used to refer to hair that goes frizzy because of humid weather even after a hair-do. *Gemince and ongedo* means 'frizzed and undone'

75

gedoek for the Wednesday biduur
                                   wearing a scarf to the Wednesday prayer meeting

joebel en juig innie gees ennie gier
                                     praise and worship as led by the spirit and emotions

purdey style	the hair-style popularized by the British actress Joanna Lumley playing the role of police officer Purdey in the TV series, *The Avengers*
kroes	frizzy
bankrot	bankrupt
Lahnie-van-Boe	the main man above; a reference to God
tjatjarag	cheeky, sassy

Pandemic piety

Tablighi	Muslim evangelist